A Really Basic Introduction to

English Law

and

The English Legal System

Michael Lambarth

© 2020

Other books available in this series include:

A Really Basic Introduction to Accountancy

A Really Basic Introduction to English Contract Law

A Really Basic Introduction to Company Law

A Really Basic Introduction to Value Added Tax

A Really Basic Introduction to Income Tax

A Really Basic Introduction to Capital Gains Tax

Contents

Chapter 1 – Introduction

Welcome to "A Really Basic Introduction to English Law". Have you ever tried to find introductory books about interesting but complicated topics, only to be completely lost after a few pages? Usually, the author starts the book by explaining how basic the book will be, and then appears to forget this altogether on the very next page when he or she starts to use technical words which you do not understand. Having stated that no previous knowledge is required, they very quickly start to assume that you know the meaning of specific terms, or they say that it would be helpful to know a bit about some other subject before reading the book. The fact that you have purchased a book which was described as a basic introduction to the subject seems to evade them completely.

This book is exactly what it says it is - a really basic introduction to English Law. No previous knowledge of law is needed or expected. I will explain everything in full as we go along and I won't try to impress you with my knowledge of complex terminology! This book will give you a good understanding of the English legal system and how it works. It will also help you if you are undertaking, or planning to undertake, any course of study where knowledge of law is required, such as law, business, management, accounting or finance. Needless to say, an introductory book of this nature does have its limitations. After reading through it, you will not understand the subject in great depth, or be able to talk to a professional adviser on their own terms. It is, after all, a really basic introduction to the topic. But it will give you a good, effective grounding in the subject which I hope will encourage you to read further into the fascinating world of law and its related subjects.

So, who am I to think that I can write such a book? Well, I am a qualified university law teacher of many years standing and a qualified solicitor. Hopefully I therefore have the skills needed to convey this subject in a clear and concise manner. I have spent a vast number of hours explaining the principles in this book to students, colleagues and clients, so I am convinced you will be able to follow what I am saying.

I have tried to keep this book as short as possible, so that it is manageable, and so that you don't lose interest or feel intimidated after just a couple of chapters. If you have ever looked for books on the law, you will have noticed that they are generally huge. This is fine for the right reader, but for someone new to the topic, it can be unnecessarily daunting. The other thing I have done is to try to keep things real and practical. Law is a difficult enough subject to grasp, without trying to do so in the abstract. Each chapter deals with different aspects and builds upon the last chapter, introducing different ideas as we go. This means that your understanding is automatically consolidated as you read and that you should be able to read this book from start to finish and end up with a pretty good understanding of what is going on. You shouldn't have to keep flicking back to previous sections to remind yourself of what you read yesterday, or last week. I hope that you will end up with a confident, basic understanding of the subject.

The law is correct as at January 2020 and many of the principles are likely to remain relevant for quite some time, but due to the changing nature of law, that is outside of my control.

I hope you enjoy the book.

Chapter 2 – Lawyers

Let's start by talking about the people involved in the legal system. There are many different labels which can be used to describe lawyers, some of which I cannot mention here! You have probably heard terms such as solicitor, barrister, advocate, attorney and judge. These words do not all have the same meaning, although we could say that they are all "lawyers". A lawyer is really just someone who works with the law. The term could extend to include academics working and researching in the law department of a university. It could also include law students.

The key terms as far as English law is concerned are solicitor, barrister and judge. An attorney is a term which is most commonly used in the United States to describe a lawyer. Attorneys generally carry out the tasks which in the UK might be split between solicitors and barristers. An advocate is really anyone who argues or speaks for a particular person or cause. In the context of the law, it usually means presenting a case to a court, which is a task undertaken by both solicitors and barristers.

A solicitor in the UK is a trained and qualified lawyer. The vast majority of solicitors will have a law degree and some form of further or vocational training received at "law school", together with a period of on-the-job training. Some solicitors may have studied a subject other than law at university and then completed a conversion course which provides them with the academic legal knowledge they need before they go on to complete their further or vocational training. (It is worth noting that from 2020, the pathways which a student will take to qualify as a solicitor are likely to change. More information on the new regime can be found on the website of the Solicitors Regulation Authority.)

Barristers take a similar path through their training, again usually starting with a law degree or a non-law degree with an additional conversion course. At this point they split from their would-be solicitor friends and whilst they also complete a stage of vocational training and a period of on-the-job training, this is different to the equivalent training undertaken by solicitors. It is therefore generally after studying a law degree or conversion course that a student of law needs to decide which branch of the legal profession they wish to enter. In practice, they might actually be applying for on-the-job training much sooner than this, whilst they are still studying for their degree.

So, what is the difference between these two roles in the English legal system? A popular way to explain it is to compare the legal profession with the medical profession. It is often said that a solicitor is like a GP and a barrister is like a consultant. In other words, a solicitor has a wide general knowledge of the law and a barrister has a deeper knowledge of a particular area of the law. A client might go to see a solicitor with what looks to be a fairly straightforward legal matter, which could turn out to be far more specialist than it first appeared, and therefore require the expertise of a barrister.

Another way that the difference in the two roles is often explained is by reference to their involvement with the court system. If someone takes a legal matter to court then they are said to be involved in litigation. Whilst it is true that a solicitor may have researched, prepared and advised upon a particular matter, generally it is a barrister who stands up before a judge and argues the case to the court. So here we can see another key difference between solicitors and barristers; barristers tend to do more court work than solicitors.

We have managed to identify two main differences between the two roles. Firstly, solicitors deal with a wide scope of work whereas barristers are more specialised. Secondly, solicitors deal with legal matters right up until the point at which they go before a court, whereas a barrister will actually present the case to the court. This latter point also necessarily means that solicitors have far more contact with the person seeking legal advice. That person will usually be the client of the solicitor and not the barrister. Historically barristers have been instructed by solicitors, on behalf of their clients, although direct access to barristers by clients is now more common than it once was.

Having said all this about the differences between the two professions, it is worth noting that things have changed quite considerably in recent years. There is far more specialisation amongst solicitors, especially in larger law firms where solicitors may well become expert in very specialist areas of legal practice. Even in smaller practices, firms tend to be split into departments with individual solicitors dealing with certain areas of specialism. In addition, many solicitors present cases to the lower courts (we'll talk more about the court system later in the book). The lower courts are the courts which tend to be the starting point for cases, rather than the higher courts which deal with more valuable or complex cases, and appeals. Many solicitors have also undertaken additional training to allow them to present cases before the higher courts.

These changes have resulted in a blurring of the line between solicitors and barristers. It is entirely possible that in the future we will see a system more like the US system in which a "lawyer" undertakes both roles, although this is probably still a good number of years away yet.

The next role in the legal profession to consider is the judge. This term can cover many roles within the legal system. The most obvious is the judge which you see at the front of a criminal courtroom on television. However, judges also hear a wide variety of other types of cases, which we will come across as we go through the book. Judges are often, but not always, legally trained in that they are usually people who used to be barristers or solicitors, often of many years standing. Some judges, such as magistrates (more on these later) are not legally trained at all and almost anyone can apply to take on that role.

For now, the important thing to note about judges is that they are not there to advise the people involved in the court case; their job is to make the final decision about who wins the case and what the outcome of that should be. In more serious criminal cases the decision of whether someone is guilty or not is not made by the judge, but by a jury made up of "ordinary" people. Even in these cases, it is the judge, not the jury, who then goes on to decide what punishment should be given. Again, we will talk more about juries later in the book.

One final role I want to mention here is that of the paralegal. The main reason for doing so is that it is a role which has become far more common in recent years than it has been in the past. Many students of law spend some time working as a paralegal on their way to qualification as a lawyer. This is because "on the job" training, to which I referred earlier as being part of the formal training for solicitors and barristers, is hard to secure. There tends to be many more students leaving universities and law schools than there are training positions in solicitors' firms and barristers' chambers. In the interim period, many students take work as paralegals to widen their experience, build contacts and help them to decide which area of law suits them best. As you can see therefore, a paralegal is generally an unqualified or part-qualified position which involves working on legal matters under the supervision of a qualified professional. They are very useful members of any legal team, and often get involved in extremely interesting and important work. It is, of course, a career in itself, and not all paralegals are students waiting to be qualified members of the professions.

In this chapter we have looked at the main "lawyers" in the English legal system. Solicitors advise clients on a variety of matters and also present some cases in court. A barrister may well have an expert knowledge in a certain area and will be trained and permitted to present cases to all courts. A judge makes decisions on cases after listening to the legal advisers present the various arguments in the case.

Chapter 3 – Criminal and Civil Law

When we think of the English legal system many of us will think about images we have seen on the television. This might be a courtroom with a judge and jury, lawyers in wigs and the person suspected of the crime sitting in the dock. It is important to appreciate that there is a key division which runs through much of the English legal system, that division being between criminal matters and civil matters.

The image referred to above from the television is that of a criminal trial. When a crime is committed, the police are usually involved in its investigation. If they find enough evidence against a person who they suspect of committing the crime, only then will they refer the case to the Crown Prosecution Service (CPS). The CPS employs lawyers who use the Code for Crown Prosecutors to work out whether it should prosecute the suspect or not. This Code requires the CPS to take into account what evidence is available and whether it is in the public interest to pursue the prosecution, based on, amongst other things, the characteristics of the offence itself. A prosecution is where someone is actually taken to court and put on trial. Many crimes are not prosecuted, often because there is simply not enough evidence to give a realistic chance of a successful prosecution. Evidence means those pieces of information that point towards someone being guilty or not guilty of the crime, such as witness statements, CCTV footage, documents, photographs and many other things. It could, for example, include a knife with blood on it.

When we think of law, a criminal case is often the first thing that comes to mind. Examples of criminal offences range from grave and serious crimes such as murder and rape, through crimes such as theft and burglary, to what are often considered to be more trivial crimes such as speeding or littering.

However, whilst the criminal law is generally the area of law which makes the headlines in our newspapers, and provides intriguing storylines for books, films and television, it is in fact a relatively small part of English law as a whole. Anything which is not a crime generally falls into a category of law called "civil law". If we think for a minute about things which are not crimes but can still be decided by the court, then we start to realise just how large and complex the body of civil law is.

Property law or land law is a hugely important area of English law for example. It has very specific rules which are different to many other countries, even Scotland. These rules tell us who owns property, what rights a person has when they rent property, how to transfer ownership of property and so on.

Whole text books have been written about the laws relating to property. If I have a dispute with my neighbour about where the boundary line falls between our properties, then this is not a criminal matter. I cannot call the police to help decide the true boundary line. If we cannot reach an agreement, then we will have to go to a civil court and ask a judge to decide.

Similarly, commercial law is a huge area of English law. This governs the relationship between parties in business. At its core it includes contract law and consumer protection law, but it also includes insurance law, company law, taxation law and laws relating to copyright, trademarks and patents to name but a few. If I buy a product from a shop and it turns out to be faulty, then again this is a civil matter and not something about which I can call the police. It is unlikely that a crime has been committed (assuming no fraud has taken place).

Finally, think of the laws relating to families. This includes the law of marriage, divorce, child protection and custody and adoption. We could also think about artificial reproduction, abortion, death and so on. In fact, the range of legal matters which are not classed as criminal matters is almost endless. There are far more lawyers working every day on these "civil" matters than there are on criminal cases. Criminal cases attract the headlines because they are exciting and interesting and more often have an impact on other people than the more private nature of civil legal matters.

In a civil matter, one person is usually suing another person. To sue someone means to take legal action against them in order to obtain a remedy, which usually consists of the payment of money or compensation, known as damages. For example, if Mr Green drives his car in such a way as to knock me off my bicycle and I can show that he was careless or negligent in doing so, then I may be able to sue him. This would involve me taking legal action against Mr Green. The law states that car drivers have a legal duty to take reasonable care not to cause injury or damage to people and objects around them. If I can show that Mr Green breached that duty and in so doing caused injury to me or damage to my bicycle, then I can sue him for what is known as negligence. Negligence on its own is not a crime and therefore the court case would be me against the driver, or "Lambarth v Green". The police and the Crown Prosecution Service would not be involved. If I win my case, then the judge is likely to order Mr Green to pay me a sum of money to compensate me for my injuries and the damage to my bicycle. Of course, Mr Green should have car insurance and so the insurance company will pay the compensation. In actual fact the insurance company is likely to take over the case on behalf of Mr Green, and if it is clear that Mr Green was at fault, the insurance company may well make an offer to pay a sum of compensation before the case goes to court. This will save the insurance company the legal costs involved and is called an "out of court settlement". Such settlements are very common in all kinds of civil cases.

So that is how a civil matter would generally proceed. Of course, in that particular case there could also be a criminal aspect. Careless driving can constitute a criminal offence, such as driving without due care and attention, and so it is possible that the police would be involved. They would try to gather sufficient evidence that Mr Green had been careless. This could consist of statements from people who had witnessed the accident, or from CCTV pictures, but also includes any injuries which I have suffered or damage caused to my bicycle. If there is enough evidence then the police might refer the matter to the Crown Prosecution Service, who will decide whether to take the matter to court. If they do, the case will be the Crown against Mr Green, or R v Green. (R here stands for Regina, Latin for "Queen".) Note that it would not be me personally who takes Mr Green to court for a criminal matter. If the court finds that Mr Green was guilty of the crime, then he would receive some kind of punishment. Criminal punishments range from community sentences through fines to imprisonment for the most serious of crimes.

The incident with the bicycle could therefore potentially give rise to two court cases. One civil case brought by me against Mr Green for compensation, and one criminal case brought by the Crown against Mr Green, probably leading to a community punishment or a fine, depending in part on how seriously I am injured.

Many civil cases do not have a criminal aspect to them. For example, if two businesses enter into a commercial contract with each other, then the breach of that contract is not something which would have any criminal aspect. If ABC Limited agrees to buy a commercial oven from XYZ Limited for £10,000 and XYZ fails to deliver the oven on time, then ABC could take them to court to seek legal redress. It would have to prove to the court that it has an agreement with XYZ in which they agreed to supply the oven by a certain date, and that the oven had not been supplied as at that date.

Once ABC Limited satisfies the court that the contract has been breached (in other words, that XYZ Limited has failed to do something it promised in the contract to do), it would need to prove how much it has lost due to the breach of contract. This is similar to what I needed to do when I sued Mr Green above. I would need to prove to the court what damage had been caused to my bicycle, and what injuries were caused to me. The courts use special tables to help them to work out how much compensation is payable for different personal injuries.

ABC Limited will need to do the same for the oven which is delivered late to it by XYZ Limited. Assuming that ABC Limited is a bakery, then it could sue XYZ Limited for any lost profit arising from the fact that it did not have a working oven for a period of time.

So far, I have focused on cases which result in a dispute which ends up in court. Lawyers do of course work on these cases. Some solicitors specialise in criminal matters and will advise clients at the police station after they are arrested, and also advise them about the court case should things proceed that far. A solicitor will often also represent the client in the early court hearings. By this I mean they will present the client's arguments to the court on behalf of the client. Should the matter be serious and continue to the higher courts, then a barrister specialising in criminal law is likely to be instructed to present the case to those higher courts. We will look more at the court system in a later chapter.

The same applies to civil matters, in that a solicitor will usually be the first port of call for someone involved in a civil dispute. Again, a barrister may be instructed to assist if the case is complex or is presented to a higher court.

Although, as I said above, I have focused on cases which end up in court, it is worth remembering that the vast majority of legal work does not involve the courts at all. Legal work which leads to a court case is referred to as "litigation" and is said to be "litigious" or "contentious". Most lawyers work in a non-contentious area of law. Let's think of some examples of non-contentious law.

Assume you want to make a will. A will is a written document which sets out a person's wishes in the event of their death. It allows a person to state to whom they want their money and possessions to go when they die. If you go to see a solicitor about making a will, you will be instructing them to work on a non-contentious matter on your behalf. You are not suing anyone, and there has been no crime. You are simply telling the solicitor that you want to make a will and the solicitor will ask you lots of questions about family members and what possessions you have and will make a note of your wishes. He or she will then draft a will reflecting those instructions and send it out to you so that you can sign it. It will then be held in a safe place until your death. The solicitor has completed their work at this point and you will no doubt have to pay for the service.

Of course, the matter might one day *become* contentious. On your death, there may be someone who feels aggrieved that you did not leave them anything in your will and they may try to contest the will. If they can prove the necessary legal elements to make such a challenge, then the matter may go to court. This would be a civil matter, but until this occurs, if ever, the matter is non-contentious.

Other areas of non-contentious work that lawyers undertake include the buying, selling and leasing of property, the formation of contracts, various types of commercial and corporate work, taxation advice, banking work, drafting terms and conditions of employment and so on. Again, the list is almost endless and includes a huge variety of work.

The point here is that whilst our everyday perception of a "lawyer" is probably that of a barrister presenting a criminal case in court, in fact the vast majority of lawyers are solicitors undertaking non-contentious work.

In this chapter we have looked at some of the differences between the criminal and civil legal systems. We have seen that the police investigate and collect evidence in a criminal matter, and then refer the case on to the Crown Prosecution Service which decides whether or not to prosecute. If they do, then the case is brought to court by the Crown against the individual defendant, and penalties include community sentences, fines and imprisonment. Civil matters are investigated by lawyers and others who they may employ to do the job. The lawyer representing the party seeking redress will help their client to decide whether to take the matter to court or not. If they do, then the case is brought against the person from whom a remedy is sought. The main remedy is an award of monetary compensation (called "damages") although other remedies can be obtained where appropriate.

Chapter 4 – Legislation

As this is an introduction to English law, we ought to consider where law originates or comes from. The most important type of law that we find in the English legal system is called legislation. Sometimes it is referred to as a "source of law" (and we'll look at some other sources of law in later chapters). A piece of legislation is also referred to as an act of Parliament or a statute. These terms all have the same meaning. This also gives a clue as to where they come from – that's right, they are produced, made or "enacted" in Parliament. Parliament in this sense consists of the House of Commons and the House of Lords, together with a final approval from the Crown called Royal Assent. The most important role is played by the House of Commons, which is what you would expect, given that the House of Commons consists of democratically elected Members of Parliament. This means, at least in theory, that we as the voting public have some say in the laws which are made in our legal system, albeit only once every five years or so at a general election.

Legislation is generally introduced to Parliament by the elected government of the day. In this way the government can legislate (produce laws) to implement its policies and in that sense law and politics are closely related. Whether the proposed legislation actually becomes law depends to some extent on whether the government has a majority of the seats in the House of Commons. A government with a large majority will be confident that its proposals will be voted through and become law. A government with a narrow majority should be able to secure the success of most of its proposals (assuming they do not upset their own Members of Parliament too much), and a government with no majority will probably need the support of members of other political parties to vote the proposals through into law.

As well as implementing its political ideals, the government may also introduce laws in response to national emergencies or particular crises (think about the 9/11 terrorist attacks on New York for example), or in response to publicity campaigns by interested groups, or simply to reform the existing law to keep it up to date.

An individual Member of Parliament can also introduce their own proposal for legislation, called a Private Members' Bill. However, these are usually done with the aim of highlighting a particular issue and a relatively low percentage of such proposals actually become law when compared to ordinary Acts of Parliament.

The first step in the life of most Acts of Parliament involves an element of consultation with experts and interested parties. This may include the production of what is known as a Green Paper, outlining the proposals and requesting the consultation. A White Paper is then produced which sets out the proposal in more detail and this is used to introduce the proposed law to Parliament. Parliamentary draftsmen then draft the proposed law, which is known as a Bill until it actually becomes law. The Bill then goes through several stages within both the House of Commons and the House of Lords, which gives Members of both Houses the chance to comment on the Bill and suggest amendments. If approved, the Bill will receive Royal Assent and become law from a certain date. Royal Assent is the approval of the Crown, but is largely a formality.

Enacting legislation in this way is a thorough but long-winded affair. The number of statutes which receive Royal Assent in a year tends to be in the region of dozens rather than hundreds. In actual fact many statutes leave the detailed provisions to be sorted out later. They provide for some other person to make the detailed regulations on particular matters. This person is often the relevant Secretary of State, and the laws made in this way are referred to as secondary or delegated legislation. The main piece of legislation is called the parent or enabling act and sets out the general scope and purpose of the secondary legislation. This secondary legislation does not then need to go through the full Parliamentary approval regime for new legislation. One of the main advantages of this type of legislation is that it can be created by people who have more expertise in the particular field than "ordinary" Members of Parliament. The regulation of financial services is an example of an area of law which utilises a vast amount of delegated legislation. Hundreds if not thousands of pieces of secondary or delegated legislation are passed into law each year, which is evidence of its wide use and importance in English law.

So now we know a little about where legislation comes from and how it is made, let's consider what it actually is. A piece of legislation is really just a list of rules, set out in numbered sections. Most commonly, those sections are numbered 1, 2, 3, 4 and so on with subsections being numbered (1), (2), (3), then (a), (b), (c) and then (i), (ii), (iii). So we might refer to section 1(3)(b)(iii) of a particular piece of legislation for example. Each piece of legislation has a name and also a year, designating the year in which it received Royal Assent. This is not always the same as the year in which it came into force as some Acts of Parliament do not have immediate effect. The Theft Act 1968 is an example of a piece of legislation. It covers many types of theft including burglary, robbery and blackmail. The various sections set out the rules relating to these offences and what must be proven in a court of law before a person can be convicted of those crimes. Lawyers working at the Crown Prosecution Service will consider the provisions carefully as part of their decision as to whether to prosecute a person who has been arrested by the police.

Another example of a piece of legislation is the Companies Act 2006. This regulates many aspects of how companies are created and operate, including financial matters. Lawyers advising companies will need to have a good working knowledge of this piece of legislation.

And so it goes on. There are thousands of pieces of legislation in English law and together they form a large chunk of the law. Lawyers and judges use these rules to decide what the law is and how it applies in any given situation. Legislation is easy to access and can generally be found online quite easily, although as it is amended by Parliament it can become more difficult to track the current version of a particular statute. Many law firms subscribe to specialist electronic databases which ensure they have access to the current law at all times.

In this chapter we have had a brief look at legislation, which makes up a significant part of English law. We have looked at where it comes from and how it is created. We have also looked at a couple of examples of statutes. It is worth noting however, that legislation is just one of a number of "sources" of English law. Another important source is case law which is established by the courts, and that is where we will turn to in the next chapter.

Chapter 5 – The Court System

Before we look in more detail at what judges do and how their decisions impact on the current law, it is important to know a little about the court structure in the English legal system. In chapter 3 we spent some time differentiating between the criminal and civil justice system, and unsurprisingly the court system is also split between these two aspects. As a general rule, civil cases are heard (decided) in what are known as the "civil courts" and criminal matters are heard in the "criminal courts". As is always the case in law, it is not quite as straightforward as that, but for our purposes we'll stick with it.

So what do we mean by the civil courts and the criminal courts? Well, let's take a criminal case first as most people tend to be more familiar with those. Assume I have stolen some goods from a shop, otherwise known as shoplifting. That is a criminal offence and if caught I will probably be arrested. I may be detained by the security personnel at the shop itself or arrested later by the police once they have tracked me down (using CCTV images and witness reports for example). If the police collect sufficient evidence then they will charge me with the offence and refer my case to the Crown Prosecution Service (which we talked about in chapter 3). They decide whether or not to prosecute me, which you will recall means take me to court. The particular court I will first appear before would be the Magistrates' Court. This is the "lowest" type of criminal court and the judge is, unsurprisingly, called a Magistrate. In fact there will usually be two or three Magistrates deciding my case. Alternatively it could be a District Judge, who is a legally qualified judge, but let's stick with Magistrates for now. Magistrates are generally not legally qualified, although they have obviously received training to equip them to do their job, and they do have a qualified clerk to advise them about legal matters should the need arise. More or less anyone can apply to be a Magistrate. The idea is that they are serving their community by administering justice to people who live in that same area. Some people think they become "case-hardened" because they deal with the same types of crimes again and again, and this gives them the reputation of being quite harsh. Whatever the truth is here, it is a fact that Magistrates deal with the vast majority of criminal cases in England and Wales.

The Magistrates' Court does, however, have limited powers. It can decide cases which are towards the less serious end of the criminal spectrum, known as summary offences. These would include littering, many driving offences, being drunk and disorderly and various technical offences relating to businesses for example. For an individual offence it can send someone to prison for up to six months (to an absolute maximum of 12 months where the defendant is convicted of two or more "either way" offences – see below). The maximum fine is unlimited, although where a very high fine is likely, consideration would be given to allocating such a case to the Crown Court – again, see below. Magistrates can also make an order that the person should undertake some kind of community sentence.

Due to the restricted sentencing powers, particularly for imprisonment, it is probably clear that they cannot decide the most serious types of offence. These are referred to as indictable offences, and would include murder, rape and robbery. In these cases, the accused will still appear before the Magistrates in the first instance, but the case will be referred on to a higher court for the full trial (or for sentencing if the accused person pleads guilty). In this case the higher court will be the Crown Court, which we will consider in a moment.

There is also a huge range of crimes which fall between minor offences and very serious offences. In fact, for many of these crimes it depends on the nature of the crime as to how serious they are. These crimes are called "either way" offences and examples include theft, drugs offences, criminal damage and burglary. Take theft for example. If I see someone accidentally drop some money on the bus and I then pick it up and treat it as my own, then this is theft. What I should do is make a reasonable effort to return the money to its owner, or simply leave it where it is of course! However, assuming the amount of money is small, then this is clearly a low level crime and, if it went to court, would be heard in the Magistrates' Court.

We could compare this to the situation where I actively go out and try to steal significant amounts of money from people's handbags when they are not looking, or where I steal a large amount of money from my employer. These crimes are likely to be treated more seriously and if the Magistrates do not feel that the appropriate punishment is within their powers then they can refer the case up to the Crown Court. The Crown Court has unlimited powers and can sentence the accused to anything up to life in prison.

You can probably see how the nature of a burglary, or of criminal damage, can determine whether a crime is heard in the Magistrates' Court or the Crown Court. A case of common vandalism is likely to end up before the Magistrates, whereas deliberately causing major structural damage to a residential building is likely to end up in the Crown Court.

When referring cases up to the Crown Court there will be a delay whilst the case is prepared and a court hearing time can be arranged. In the meantime there is the question of what will happen to the accused. This is another task of the Magistrates' Court – to decide if bail should be granted. If bail is granted then the accused is free to go pending the Crown Court hearing. Strict bail conditions might be applied by the court, such as the accused being ordered to surrender their passport or refrain from contacting certain people or going to specified places. Bail can also be an issue if the court needs to wait for further information to be produced before it can decide punishment, such as a report from a social worker.

The Crown Court itself differs to the Magistrates' Court. In the Crown Court we will always find a qualified judge, as well as a jury. There is no jury in the Magistrates' Court and so the Magistrates themselves determine the guilt of the accused and then decide on any appropriate punishment. In the Crown Court it is the jury which decides whether a person is guilty. A basic jury consists of 12 people drawn at random from the general population and, like a Magistrate, is an example of the legal system using lay-people (unqualified people) to undertake an important role. The job of the jury is to assess the evidence presented by both the accused (known as the defendant) and by the prosecution. The role of the judge is to ensure that the trial is fair and to decide what punishment should be applied if and when it is necessary. The judge will apply the rules of evidence so that the jury only gets to evaluate evidence which is fair. These rules are complex but essential to ensure that justice is done.

The jury can only convict the defendant if they decide that he or she is guilty beyond reasonable doubt. This is a very high level of proof. It means that the members of the jury must have no doubt in their minds that the defendant is guilty. The evidence must therefore be reliable and credible in order to persuade the jury of the defendant's guilt. If the defendant is found not guilty then they are free to go. If they are found guilty then the judge will pass sentence. Unlimited fines and life sentences are available to Crown Court judges, although each type of offence brings its own limitations on sentencing. Murder carries a mandatory life sentence (although this does not necessarily mean that the guilty person will spend the rest of their life in prison).

Many people who are new to the study of law find the concept of evidence quite difficult. When all is said and done, it is not about what happened, but about what can be evidenced – what does the proof suggest? Undoubtedly people are not prosecuted, or not found guilty, of crimes they have committed because there is not enough evidence to convict them. Similarly, innocent people are sometimes found guilty because evidence is misunderstood or falsified in some way. The not perfect, but if we start advocating a system in which people can be found guilty just because "we know" they are guilty, we are starting out on a very dangerous road. Appeal processes are there to correct miscarriages of justice, and we'll look at those a little later on.

So the first two criminal courts we have encountered are the Magistrates' Court and the Crown Court. Let's turn our attention to the civil court system for a while. Remember, the civil courts hear or decide cases which are not criminal; in other words, cases which do not include a crime. We said in chapter 3 that this in fact amounts to a massive body of law and therefore a huge number of cases each year, including contract and commercial cases, family matters, cases about land and property, personal injury and so on.

The lowest civil court is called the County Court. Like Magistrates' Courts, they are spread around England and Wales in all major towns and cities. The majority of civil cases will start in the County Court, although some "larger" or more complex cases can be started in the High Court depending on the nature of the case.

Cases in the County Court are heard by a circuit judge or a district judge. Both are legally qualified and work on their own. A circuit judge also hears cases in the Crown Court, and tends to hear the more complex cases in the County Court. Judges try to keep civil cases moving so that they are dealt with quickly and efficiently. There tends to be more toing and froing in and out of court in civil matters due to the variety of cases which arise and the complexity of the particular issues at stake. One of the parties to the dispute might want to slow things down and that is something the courts do not like to see. Remember that in a civil case it is generally one person against another, unlike a criminal case where the Crown Prosecution Service prosecutes the defendant on behalf of the Crown.

There is no jury in civil cases. Exceptions do exist, the main one being for cases involving defamation (where someone tells lies about someone else which damage their character) but the vast majority of civil cases will be heard without a jury. The judge will therefore assess the evidence and the legal arguments of both parties to the case and then make a decision about who has the better case. Rather than having to decide beyond reasonable doubt as in criminal cases, the level here is on the balance of probabilities. This simply means that the judge will decide in favour of the person who has the strongest case. As we said earlier, the parties are usually looking for monetary compensation or some other order of the court (the return of some property for example, or an order to stop trespassing on land). Some civil cases lead to specialist remedies. For example, a local authority might approach the civil courts for what is known as a care order. A care order is an order of the court to the effect that a child should be placed into the care of the local authority, usually to protect them from potential harm. The variety of civil cases means that the range of potential outcomes from a civil case is wide.

Evidence is still a key component of civil cases, as it is of criminal cases. If I want the court to order someone to pay me a debt they owe me, then I have to prove that such a debt exists and that it has not yet been paid. If I can do this sufficiently well to tip the balance in my favour so that the judge is minded to grant the order, then the other party will need to produce evidence that no such debt ever existed, or that it has been paid, or that there is some other good reason why the court should not order that the debt now be paid. Evidence can consist of anything which helps to prove to the court that what you are saying is true. It can include CCTV images, witness statements, photographs, medical reports, expert reports, documentary evidence and so on. For my debt case, I will want to produce any written agreement we had between us, or any order forms, statements or invoices which prove the amount outstanding. The other party might produce a copy of a cheque or electronic payment or possibly any receipt they have received to evidence the fact that they have paid.

The High Court, which hears civil cases that are more complex or involve larger amounts of money, is presided over by a High Court judge. Again, these judges are legally qualified and usually hear cases alone. The High Court is split into three divisions which cover different areas of law. They are known as the Family Division, the Chancery Division and the Queen's Bench Division.

Unsurprisingly, the Family Division decides cases relating to family issues such as marriage, children and death. The Chancery Division decides cases about tax, bankruptcy, patents, trusts and disputes involving companies. Finally, the Queen's Bench Division hears cases on contractual disputes, commercial matters and general civil matters such as claims for personal injury. Being a civil court, the High Court has no jury of course.

At this point let's just remind ourselves of something we said earlier in the book. In chapter 2 we were talking about the difference between a solicitor and a barrister and we highlighted one of the main differences being that a barrister tends to do more court work than a solicitor. In fact, solicitors are generally allowed to present cases in the two lower courts that we have just been discussing, being the Magistrates' Court for criminal matters and the County Court for civil matters. If the case proceeds higher, to the Crown Court or High Court, then a barrister would need to be instructed to present the case to the court, unless the solicitor had undergone specialist training to enable them to present before the higher courts.

It is worth noting that civil cases generally must follow a certain procedure and that procedure depends on the track to which the case is allocated. This happens before the court hearing. Claims under £10,000 are usually allocated to the small claims track. The procedure is simple, and the hearing usually occurs reasonably quickly (usually in months rather than years). Fast track claims are generally between £10,000 and £25,000 and last no longer than one day, with the hearing often coming within a year. Finally, multi-track claims are for the larger and more complex claims and the hearing will often take more than a day and may not come to court for a year or two.

Once we get above the Crown Court and the High Court, the criminal and civil systems sort of come together in that the next step up the ladder for both the criminal and civil systems is the Court of Appeal. You are likely to have heard about this on the news. The Court of Appeal hears important cases which often have some kind of national interest. It is split into two divisions, being the criminal and civil divisions. Court of Appeal judges are very senior judges and tend to sit three at a time to hear a case. The Court only hears appeals, so they will always be cases which have already been heard by a lower court. In fact, the Crown Court and High Court also hear appeals from the courts below them (the Magistrates' Court and the County Court), but most of their time is spent hearing new cases. The Court of Appeal is the first court we have met which deals solely with appeals.

Finally, at least within England and Wales, we find the UK Supreme Court sitting at the top of the ladder of the court system. This court hears appeals from the Court of Appeal in both civil and criminal matters, and sometimes from the High Court. Its functions used to be undertaken by the House of Lords. Like the Court of Appeal, senior judges decide cases in this court and they tend to sit in fives, or even sevens for very important cases. A majority verdict is needed to reach a decision and it is not uncommon for the judges to be split 3:2 in complex or controversial cases.

When it comes to appeals, they are usually heard by the court which is next "up the chain" in the court system. For example, an appeal from a decision made in a County Court will usually be heard in the

High Court. An appeal is the right of a person to challenge the decision that has been made by the court. Obviously, it is usually the person who has lost the court case who will appeal. If the appeal is successful then the decision of the original court is replaced by the decision of the new, higher court.

So there we have a brief summary of the court system in England and Wales as well as the appeal process. There are other types of court which I have not included here in order to keep things simple. For example, you may well have heard of tribunals. These are a type of court found towards the lower end of the court system and tend to deal with specialist areas such as social security matters, employment disputes and taxation cases. It is also worth noting here that many people decide that the court system is not for them and they seek some form of alternative dispute resolution outside the court system. Our next task is to think about what it is that the courts actually do and how this helps to develop English law.

Chapter 6 – The Common Law

In the previous chapter we looked at the court system and saw that there is a hierarchy, with lower courts at the "bottom" of the chain such as the Magistrates' Court and the County Court, leading up through the Crown Court and High Court to the Court of Appeal and the Supreme Court. The question for us to think about now is what it is that the courts do that is so important in terms of developing English law.

The starting point is to think back to chapter 4 which was about legislation. In that chapter we saw that most new law is made in Parliament and a law made in this way is referred to as a piece of legislation or a statute or an act of Parliament.

However, there are many laws that exist today that are not based on any legislation. One of the most obvious is the law of murder. There is no "Murder Act" in the same way as there is a "Theft Act". The Theft Act 1968 tells us what the law is on theft and covers various different types of theft. It explains what the requirements are for those offences and what punishments the courts can order if someone is found guilty. Murder, on the other hand, is what we call a common law offence. This means it has been created and developed by the courts over the course of hundreds of years. Murder generally occurs where someone causes the death of another person and either intends to kill them or intends to inflict very serious harm. These are terms which the courts have defined and re-defined over the years as cases of murder have come before them. Each case brings its own set of facts and judges apply the law to each case as it arises and new or unusual factual scenarios may result in the definitions being changed or expanded or otherwise modified in some way. Another example of a common law offence is common assault. The Law Commission, which is a body set up by Parliament to keep English law under review, has a programme to legislate for each common law offence in order to try to clarify some of the vagaries of those offences. In other words the intention is to pass a piece of legislation through Parliament to cover each offence, setting out clearly what the requirements are for each such offence.

Moving away from the criminal law to the civil law, a good example of an area of law which relies heavily on the common law is contract law. This body of law governs how contracts are made and how they can be broken, together with the remedies which are available to someone who suffers a breach of contract. Again, there is no "Contract Law Act" and so the majority of the rules remain "hidden" in the case decisions made by judges. Parts of the law of contract can be found in various pieces of legislation, but generally the law of contract is founded in common law.

We have looked at a couple of examples of major areas of law which are grounded in common law, but how does this actually work? The answer is that as each case is decided by the courts it adds to the body of rules in that area. Clearly there may be many cases about contract law each year, and there may be many (though hopefully fewer) cases about murder. Not every case will change or add to the law however. That is due to the system of precedent, which is key to English law.

The system of precedent basically means that a court must consider the decisions made in previous court cases. If a court has already decided that it is an offence for a man to rape his wife (as it did in *R v R* (1992)), then if the same situation comes before the court again, the court must generally follow the previous ruling. This ensures that the system is fair and applied equally in each case; it gives the advantage of consistency.

There are a few things to note about this system however. Firstly, it is generally the higher courts which set the precedents in the first place. Decisions made in the highest court, the Supreme Court, bind all lower courts. That means that the Court of Appeal (Criminal Division), the Crown Courts and the

Magistrates' Courts all need to follow the principle decided in the Supreme Court decision if it is a criminal matter. If it is a civil matter, then the Court of Appeal (Civil Division), the High Courts and the County Courts will all need to follow the decision. A decision in the Court of Appeal similarly binds all courts below it, and in most cases will also bind future Court of Appeal decision (with some exceptions). Lower down the hierarchy, High Court decisions can bind the County Court but the County Court itself, and the Crown Court and Magistrates' Court cannot generally make a decision which binds any future court.

The second thing to note about the system of precedent is that it is not the whole case that sets a precedent. Only the main legal principle coming out of the case will become part of the precedent which is then set for other cases to follow. Judges tend to write fairly long judgments when they decide important cases in higher courts. Not everything they say becomes a precedent and it is the job of a skilled lawyer to pick out from that judgment the particular principles that form the precedent. It is these principles which then build, develop and change the law as the years go by. Judges can only decide on cases that actually come before them, and can therefore only influence the law when a suitable and relevant case appears in their court. There may be areas of law which judges would like to amend, but they have no mechanism for doing so until and unless a relevant case comes before them. The common law, made up of a series of case decisions which bind other courts, therefore develops in a rather piecemeal fashion. This can be contrasted to legislation which Parliament can change at any time by passing a new piece of legislation. It is also worth noting here that Parliament can of course pass a piece of legislation at any time to change the common law positon. For example, if it does not like the way that the law of murder is being developed by the courts, it could pass a Murder Act to change it. The courts have no power to change what is set down clearly in legislation. In this way we can see that Parliament is the supreme law making body for England and Wales.

Another point to keep in mind about the system of precedent is that judges can use the facts of a case to reach a different result. Two cases which at first sight appear to be very similar may in fact involve significant factual differences and therefore a judge can *distinguish* one case from the other. That means that whilst there has been an earlier case which has set a precedent about a particular legal point, a judge in a later case might be able to avoid applying that principle to that later case on the basis that the facts are significantly different. This allows judges some flexibility in how they apply the law in their aim to do justice to the people involved in the case. A higher court can, of course, simply overrule a decision from a previous case which was decided by a lower court. This would have the effect of removing that precedent from the law and replacing it with the new decision from the higher court.

Finally on the general system of precedent, it is clear that the body of case decisions (case law) which has built up over the past several hundred years is huge. There are literally thousands and thousands of precedents in hundreds of different areas of law on all kinds of legal issues. Working out what the law is can therefore be problematic. It is essential to have a very clear method of law reporting. A law report is a report of a case, consisting mainly of the judgment as written or delivered by the judge or judges in the case. Finding the current law is a task which has, thankfully, vastly improved by the use of electronic databases. Searches on these databases using appropriate keywords will usually bring up a list of the relevant cases fairly quickly, although that is a skill in itself and some knowledge of the relevant legal area will obviously help with that.

The final issue I want to look at in this chapter is the task of statutory interpretation. Whilst it is true that statutes produced by Parliament go through a fairly rigorous process before they receive Royal Assent, it is true that many pieces of legislation contain provisions which are open to interpretation. Everyday words such as "building" or "vehicle" can cause problems. Is a caravan a building or a vehicle? What about a boat? Is a tent a building? If legislation were drafted to include a full definition of every term used, then it would be unimaginably long and probably very difficult to read or use.

Another important role of judges is therefore to interpret what is meant by a particular phrase in a piece of legislation. Many cases come before the courts which require this exercise to be undertaken. A classic example often used here is the case of *Brock v DPP* (1993). This focused on the meaning of the words "type of pit bull terrier" used in the Dangerous Dogs Act 1991. The court was required to decide whether the word "type" had the same meaning as "breed". If so, then only pit bull terriers were covered by the particular provision. The court actually decided that the word "type" had a wider meaning than just including a breed, and so other dogs, with similar characteristics as a pit bull terrier could be covered by the legislation. You can see how this would be important to someone charged with an offence under the Act who owned a dog which was a similar type to a pit bull terrier but not actually of that breed. The court's decision meant that such a person could be guilty of the offence.

Students new to the study of law often get confused by statutory interpretation. That is probably because teachers often deal with it separately to the system of precedent that we have already looked at. However, it is really just part and parcel of that system. It is still true that judges can only become involved in interpretation when a relevant case comes before them. It is also true that any decision made by the court will then form a precedent to bind lower courts in the usual way.

There are rules of interpretation that judges consider when trying to establish the meaning of words. The first rule is called the literal rule, and as you would expect, it means that judges look at the literal meaning of the words used in the statute. That means they give the words their ordinary or everyday meaning or, if you prefer, their dictionary definition. *Fisher v Bell* (1960) is the case most often used as an example here. It is an offence to offer a flick-knife for sale. However, in law, placing an item in a shop window is not technically "offering" it for sale, it simply invites others to make an offer to buy the item. The court therefore found that the accused was not guilty of offering the knife for sale when he placed it in his shop window; the court interpreted the wording of the statue very literally.

So the starting point used by many judges is to try the ordinary meaning of the words used in the statute. However, this can give rise to some rather absurd results on occasion. The case of *Alder v George* (1964) is a good example. The Official Secrets Act 1920 made it an offence to obstruct HM Armed Forces in the vicinity of a prohibited place. The accused argued that he was in fact *in* the prohibited place (an air force base) rather than "in the vicinity" of it. On a literal interpretation of the words used, he would not be guilty of an offence. However, the court applied what is known as the golden rule of interpretation, which states that if the literal rule leads to an absurd result, then some other interpretation should be used instead. The court thought the outcome of this case was absurd, and so decided that "in the vicinity" of a place included "in the place itself" and found him guilty.

Other rules of statutory interpretation include the mischief rule and the purposive approach. Both of these rules allow the court to look not at the exact meaning of the words, but at the gap in the law that the particular statute is trying to fill, and also at what it feels Parliament was trying to achieve when it passed the law. In other words, the court uses the interpretation which satisfies the objective or intention behind why the law was created in the first place. An often quoted example is the case of *Smith v Hughes* (1960). This required an interpretation of a phrase in the Street Offences Act 1959. The phrase made it an offence to "loiter or solicit in the street for the purposes of prostitution". The accused claimed that they were not "in the street" because they were generally on balconies or knocking on windows from within buildings. The court used the mischief rule to deem that such behaviour occurred "in the street" because the intention behind the legislation was to prevent prostitutes harassing people in the street, and this is what they were doing.

We have seen in this chapter that the courts have a very important part to play in the development of English law. The decisions made in higher courts become binding precedents and subsequent cases in lower courts must follow those decisions when based on similar facts. Included in this role is the important job of interpreting the meaning of legislation as and when required. Decisions made as to how a word or phrase applies in a particular factual situation, or as to its scope or extent, also bind courts which are lower in the hierarchy.

Chapter 7 – The European Union

Whilst this book is a really basic introduction to English law and the English legal system, it would not be complete without some consideration of its relationship with the European Union.

The general concept of the union of Europe stems back to the time after the Second World War and a desire amongst European countries not to see a repeat of the horrors which took place. Through a series of treaties we now have a European Union which consists of a number of bodies. The general idea is that there should be economic harmonisation across member countries of the European Union in order to create a fair and equal market place for business to thrive. For example, laws on issues such as consumer protection, employment and some areas of taxation are determined to a large extent by European laws.

No doubt you will have heard about Members of the European Parliament standing for election; you might even have voted in those elections at some point. You will probably also have heard of the European Court of Justice, the European Council (once called the Council of Ministers) and the European Commission. Between them these bodies have the power to create European laws which potentially have an impact on all countries which are members of the European Union. Since the United Kingdom is a member of the European Union, these laws have an important impact on English law.

We have seen in chapter 4 that the UK Parliament in London is supreme when it comes to making English law. In other words, it has the power to make or change any law, including laws developed by judges (which we considered in chapter 6 as being the common law). So how does European law fit with this concept that Parliament is supreme?

The answer is that Parliament has voluntarily given up its right of supremacy in relation to European laws. The European Communities Act 1972 was passed by the UK Parliament and this act incorporated European law into English law. For now the Act is in force and therefore England and Wales are voluntarily subject to the laws created by the European Union. However, that Act could be repealed at any time, which means that Parliament retains overall supremacy.

Law is made in the European institutions referred to above. Proposals come from the European Commission, sometimes following a request from the European Council. Approval for any new laws must be given by the European Parliament, although this role is shared with the European Council. A common criticism of the process is that the

European Parliament should have more powers considering it is the only directly elected body involved in the process.

The other way that law is developed in Europe is through the decisions of the European Court of Justice which are generally binding on all countries in the European Union. They often relate to the interpretation of other European laws and help to ensure consistency of application across all member countries.

The most important types of law which come from the European Union are treaties, regulations, directives, decisions, recommendations and opinions and we will now look very briefly at each of these in turn.

Treaties are the headline agreements between the various member countries of the European Union. They create the institutions of the European Union which we have referred to above such as the European Parliament and the European Council; they also give those institutions their powers.

The laws actually created by the institutions themselves include regulations. These are the most "powerful" types of law in that they are applicable in themselves in every member country of the European Union. In other words, as soon as they come into force they become part of English law and must be followed by those who are covered by the law.

A European directive is another type of law created by the European Union. This differs from a regulation in that a directive generally needs to be implemented by the legal system of each country. In other words, it is really an instruction to each country to change their laws to the extent necessary to ensure that a particular legal position is reached. They are commonly used as they are an effective way to ensure that the law is consistent throughout the member countries of the European Union, which will usually be given a time limit within which to implement the provisions of the directive.

Decisions are binding only on the person or country to which they relate, rather than across the whole European Union. Recommendations and opinions are not binding and are therefore less effective as legal measures.

European law is a vast and important part of English law. Many areas of law include some aspects of European law and therefore it is important to be aware of its existence. A good example is Value Added Tax (or VAT for short). I'm sure you will have heard of VAT as being a tax which we pay when we purchase goods and services. VAT law stems from a European Directive. That directive required member countries to implement the laws relating to VAT into their own legal systems. The English law version can be found in the Value Added Tax Act 1994. This is a "normal" statute passed by Parliament in the usual way. However, when interpreting that statute, it is a good idea to look back at the original directive from Europe to help to understand what the law is trying to achieve. The result overall is that VAT law is more or less the same in all countries of the European Union.

Of course we should not finish this chapter without a mention of the United Kingdom's referendum to leave the European Union. On 23 June 2016 the public voted to leave the EU. This means in its simplest form, that the European Communities Act 1972 will be repealed and Parliament will once again be supreme in the sense that it will no longer have given up voluntary power to the EU institutions. Of course, in practice the process is proving to be complex and there are many legal implications. As we have seen above, many laws which have been created in Europe have now been implemented into English law, and those laws, at least for the time being, will remain in force. Others will need to be incorporated into English law after "Brexit" if we wish them to remain in force. Only time will tell exactly how this will be achieved and how effective it will be. Away from the legal complexities, leaving the

European Union has also tested the political institutions of the UK. Many politicians appreciate that they have at least a moral duty to follow the result of the referendum, but it is proving difficult to agree on exactly what is the best way to achieve that. Following the December 2019 general election, it now seems that the UK will leave the Union on 31 January 2020. Even after this date, negotiations will continue to establish the ongoing relationship between the UK and the European Union.

We have seen in this chapter that European law has had a major impact on UK law and English law in particular. We have looked briefly at the institutions of the European Union and the various types of law which they can make. There is another important aspect of European law which we will now go on to consider, and that is the issue of Human Rights.

Chapter 8 – Human Rights

A human right is a right which we are entitled to simply because we are human. Most people would agree that included in that category are rights such as the right to life, the right to a fair trial, the right to practise any religion we choose, the right to free speech and the right to live free from torture. There are plenty of other examples too.

The law relating to human rights is an area which is influenced to a large degree by Europe, and this is another of those issues which can cause confusion to those that are new to the study of law. The confusion stems from the fact that European "laws" on human rights are not related to the European Union system that we looked at in the previous chapter. There we saw that the European Union can make laws which have an impact on the UK and other member countries. These tend to relate to economic activity rather than human rights. The European Court of Justice that we mentioned briefly deals with issues which arise from the laws created by the European Union, not human rights. The European dimension of human rights comes out of the European Convention on Human Rights and cases about human rights are dealt with in the European Court of Human Rights. These things are not related to the European Union institutions.

Much like the general concept of the union of Europe, the European Convention on Human Rights was developed after the Second World War with the aim of avoiding a repetition of the horrors that had occurred at that time. Drafted in 1950, it came into force in 1953 and sets out those fundamental human rights we talked about earlier. In addition, it includes rights relating to privacy, education, marriage and discrimination amongst others. Rights have been added to it in the years since it was originally drafted.

An important feature of the European Convention on Human Rights is that for many years it was not strictly part of English law. Judges could refer to it in the courts and use it to help them interpret statutory provisions if they thought it was helpful to do so, but it generally played a limited part in English law. An individual who thought their human rights were being denied in some way could take their case to the European Court of Human Rights, but this was generally a slow and costly process.

This changed to an extent with the introduction in 2000 of the Human Rights Act 1998. This legislation was passed by the UK Parliament and paved the way for human rights to take on a more established role in English law. The main changes made were that English courts can now give a remedy to someone who has suffered the breach of a "convention right", which is a human right from the European Convention on Human Rights which has been given some effect in English law by the Human Rights Act 1998. This in turn means that individuals no longer need to take their case to the European Court of Human Rights to get the justice they seek.

In addition, English courts must now interpret legislation to be in line with the convention rights wherever possible. Note however, that they cannot override UK legislation if it is contrary to those convention rights. What they can do in that instance is make a declaration that the particular piece of legislation is not compatible with the convention rights and this will often lead to a change in the law by Parliament. Finally, the courts must also now take into account decisions and opinions of the European Court of Human Rights.

It is fair to say that the issue of human rights is an area of law that has proved to be hugely controversial. Whilst most people would not dispute the importance of such rights, many would argue that English law has sufficient mechanisms within it to protect those rights without the need for reference to the European Convention. After all, English law already contains laws which prevent us from suffering torture, protecting our privacy to some degree, allowing us to marry, safeguarding our freedom of expression within reasonable limits and so on. On the other hand, the number of cases which came before the European Court of Human Rights before 2000 and the number of times the 1998 Act has been implemented by the courts since 2000 suggests all is not rosy in the garden. As always, the true position is no doubt somewhere in the middle; the Convention and the 1998 Act have no doubt helped to ensure the protection of human rights, but there is also a danger that the courts take some of the provisions a little too far in some cases.

In this chapter we have looked at human rights and how they are protected. Remember that this is a separate issue to the European Union system and the European Court of Justice. If I have say, a value added tax dispute, then I might end up appealing the decision right up to the European Court of Justice on a point of law if it is important enough. The European Convention on Human Rights and the European Court of Human Rights are there to protect my human rights, for example if I felt that my freedom to practise my religion was being compromised. It is important to appreciate the difference between these two aspects of European law.

Chapter 9 – Core Subjects: Contract law

Now that we have looked at the English legal system, we can move on to consider some of the key areas of English law. The first area I have chosen is contract law. The reason for this is that it is a subject which tends to be taught in the first year of a law degree course and is a central part of many other legal qualifications and it is also fundamental to many other areas of law. For example, most commercial transactions are based on contract law, as are consumer transactions, banking deals and property transactions amongst others. All these things involve a contract and it is therefore essential to have a basic grasp of the issues. A book of this nature can do no more than give a very brief introduction to the topic. There are plenty of other books available which will help you further your study of contract law, such as the excellent "A Really Basic Introduction to English Contract Law" (!)

English contract law is largely a common law subject. We talked earlier in the book about some areas of law being formed and developed by a series of case decisions made by judges, and contract law is one of those areas. There are some relevant statutes, many of which cover consumer protection issues, but many of the key rules stem from the decisions of judges. It is also a civil law topic, rather than criminal law. That means that disputes that go to court are resolved in the civil court system that we looked at earlier. Court action will therefore generally be started in the County Court or possibly in the High Court.

English contract law is based on agreement. In other words, we choose to enter into a contract or not. Only when we have committed to such an act do contractual obligations become binding on us. It is worth noting at this stage that a legally binding contract can be entered into in writing or it can be made orally – by spoken words. The advantage of writing is that it provides a record of what was actually contained in the agreement. Oral contracts can be problematic when it comes to proving what was agreed in the first place.

For a contract to exist the courts have said that there needs to be an offer made by one party to the contract which is then accepted by the other party. The offer should set out all the terms which the person making the offer is willing to agree to in the contract. The other party should then simply accept those terms without further amendment. We make offers like this every day. When I go into a shop to buy something, the courts have said that I am offering to buy the product and that the shop accepts my offer by recording the sale at the counter and accepting my money. This was confirmed in the case of *Pharmaceutical Society of Great Britain v*

Boots Cash Chemists (Southern) Limited (1952). The court said that a display of goods in a shop is generally an invitation to treat and not an offer for sale. This means the shop is inviting the customer to make an offer, which the shop can then accept or decline as it chooses. It also means that if a shop mistakenly prices goods too low, we cannot force them to sell at that lower price, despite popular belief to the contrary!

As well as an offer and an acceptance, there are a few other requirements which the courts look for to create a legally binding contract. The first of those is a concept known as "consideration". Once again this is something which tends to cause some confusion to those new to the subject. Consideration has been defined by the courts in various cases. One of the most well-known is the case of *Currie v Misa* (1875) in which the court defined consideration as a right or benefit accruing to one party or a loss or detriment suffered by the other. An obvious example of consideration is the price paid under a contract for the purchase of goods or services. For the contract to be valid, both parties generally need to provide consideration and that means that the promise of a gift or to do something for "free" is generally not legally binding. If I agree with the window cleaner that he will clean my windows for £10, then the consideration I give is the £10. That is both to his benefit and to my detriment. The consideration he provides is that he cleans my windows, therefore giving up his time, skill and presumably, his cleaning products. That is to his detriment and to my benefit, therefore satisfying the definition of a valid consideration.

It is fair to say that consideration is a controversial topic. Some lawyers believe that it is unnecessary and that tests based on whether the parties intended to be bound by the contract are enough to sidestep the need for consideration. Indeed, many other legal jurisdictions in the world do not have such a concept. The courts are still trying to sort out exactly what is included within the definition and it is a concept which gives judges scope to be "creative" in their search for justice.

The next thing judges look for in their search for a binding contract is certainty. The original offer should contain all the terms of the contract, and the other party should just be able to accept it. Those terms need to be clear and all-encompassing. It should be apparent to anyone "looking in" at the contracting stage what the terms of the contract are and what they mean.

The courts do have some scope for implying terms into a contract, which means that they can decide that a clause exists in a contract even though the parties did not actually include it when they entered into the contract. However, they are generally reluctant to do so due to the doctrine of freedom of contract. This doctrine provides that people are free to enter into contracts as they choose and they should be bound by what they have agreed to do. Having said this, the courts will on occasion imply a term into a contract to make the contract work in the way that the court thinks the parties intended it to work.

The final basic requirement for a valid and binding contract is intention. What this means is that the parties must have intended to be legally bound by the contract. The test is whether they appeared to intend to be bound, rather than that they actually intended to be bound. The courts do not therefore ask the parties whether they intended to be legally bound, they look at their words and conduct to see if a "reasonable" person would think they so intended. There are two presumptions which the courts make to help them assess the case before them.

Firstly, they assume that people who make agreements in a social or domestic setting do not intend to be legally bound by that agreement. This can be seen in operation in the case of *Balfour v Balfour* (1919) in which the court decided that an agreement between husband and wife was not binding.

Secondly, they assume that people who make agreements in a business or commercial setting *do* intend to be legally bound by the agreement. An example is the case of *Esso Petroleum Co. Ltd v Commissioners of Customs and Excise* (1976).

Now we have considered briefly the way that contracts are made, we should look at how they can come to an end or, to use the technical term, how they are discharged. The obligations that two parties owe to each other under a contract can come to an end in a variety of ways. The most obvious is by performance of those obligations in accordance with the contract. If I employ a decorator to paint my dining room, then the contract will come to a natural end when the decorator has finished painting my dining room to an acceptable standard and I have paid the money I owe under the contract. The obligations that we both had have been performed as envisaged in our contract and so it has now ended.

Another way that the contract may come to an end is by agreement. This could be before performance has started. For example, if the decorator telephones me to say that he is not very well and will not be able to complete the job for a few weeks, then we may agree to release each other from our respective obligations. I agree that he does not need to decorate my dining room and he agrees that I do not need to pay him.

Another method by which a contract is discharged is through "frustration". A contract becomes frustrated when it becomes impossible to perform or when performance becomes something very different to what was envisaged when the contract was entered into. Generally the circumstance which alters things must be something which was outside the control of the contracting parties. The common example used to explain frustration is the case of *Taylor v Caldwell* (1863). In that case an agreement for the hire of a concert hall was frustrated when the concert hall burnt down in a fire which was not the fault of either party to the contract. You can see that the contract could no longer be performed as agreed because the concert hall no longer existed. It therefore effectively comes to an end.

Along with full performance of the contract, perhaps the most important way in which a contract can come to an end is due to a breach of contract. This is where one party to the contract fails to perform their contractual obligations as agreed. Let's look at an example to round off this chapter, which we can also use to cover the remedies available when a breach of contract occurs.

Davina runs her own bakery business and contacts Ed, a local ingredient supplier. He offers to supply ingredients to Davina on the first working day of each month for the next 12 months for a fixed price of £300 per month, payable within seven days of each delivery. Davina agrees with these terms and so accepts his offer.

As a reminder, this amounts to a valid contract. Ed made an offer containing the terms of the contract, which Davina accepted. The terms were certain (let's assume the detail of what exactly was being delivered was agreed), and both parties clearly provided the necessary consideration; Ed has promised to deliver baking ingredients, and Davina has promised to pay £300 for them each month. There is also an intention to create legal relations. This is a business or commercial transaction and therefore a court would assume that the parties intended to be legally bound by their actions.

Everything goes to plan for the first three months of the contract which sees Ed deliver good quality produce and Davina paid for them as agreed. However, in the fourth month Ed's delivery is a few days late. Davina agrees to overlook this and pays for the ingredients as usual. On the fifth month, Ed's delivery is three weeks late and Davina is now considering her options.

In contract law terms, what we saw for the first three months of the contract was full performance by both parties. In other words, they were both doing what they agreed to do. Had they continued to behave in this way, the contract would have run its course and ended after 12 months; the obligations of the parties would have been discharged by performance. However, in month four it appears that Ed breached his side of the bargain. He did deliver the produce to Davina but it was late. Note that the reasons why it was late are not generally relevant; he promised to deliver on the first working day of each month and he did not do that, therefore he breached the contract.

The first thing to note about a breach of contract is that it always gives the "innocent" party a right to claim damages (compensation) for any losses caused by the breach. Therefore Davina could, after the late delivery in the fourth month, have taken Ed to court and sued him for any losses she could show had arisen. For example, if she had run out of ingredients and could therefore not do any baking for a few days, she may well lose out on orders from her own customers. If so, she could sue for the lost profit from those orders. In reality, minor breaches of contracts occur very often. Assuming Davina carries a stock of ingredients and therefore had enough left over from the previous month, she probably wouldn't lose out and therefore is content to accept Ed's apology and leave it at that. Even if it caused her some inconvenience and a lost sale or two she may still choose not to take any further action. She could try to settle things without going to court, perhaps by asking for a reduction in the price for that month to reflect the fact that the delivery was late.

When it comes to the fifth month, Ed's delivery is three weeks late. This is clearly a much more serious breach of the same term of the contract than when he was a few days late. It may well be that Davina will want to bring the contract to an end now because she thinks that Ed will continue to deliver late and it will no doubt cause problems to her business.

Whether she can do this or not depends on what kind of term has been breached. In law there is an important distinction between contractual terms which are classed as "conditions" and contractual terms which are classed as "warranties". A condition is a term of the contract which goes to the heart of what the contract is about. In other words, it is a key contractual term involving an important aspect of the contract. A warranty is a term which is less important and not central to the main purpose of the contract.

The importance of the distinction between conditions and warranties is in the remedy which is available.

The breach of a warranty allows the other party to sue for damages (compensation), whereas the breach of a condition allows the other party to terminate the contract.

So what type of clause is the delivery clause? This could conceivably be a condition, especially if Davina has highlighted it as being particularly important for good reasons (such as the fact that she tended to run her stock right down to nothing each month to keep things fresh). It is probably unlikely to be a warranty because it is certainly of some importance, which brings us to the third and final classification of contractual terms, known as "innominate terms". This idea was developed in the case of *Hong Kong Fir Shipping Limited v Kawasaki Kisen Kaisha* (1962) and refers to a contractual term which is somewhere between a warranty and a condition. It is basically a term, the status of which really depends on the nature and effect of the actual breach that occurs. As we have seen in Davina's case, Ed could breach the delivery term by a very short period which may not have too much effect on her business. On the other hand he could breach it quite significantly (the fifth month delivery is now three weeks late) and this could have a serious impact on her business.

If the delivery clause is an innominate term, then the breach in the fourth month is probably only going to lead to a claim for compensation (in fact Davina overlooked the breach entirely) and the breach in the fifth month may well give rise to a right to terminate the contract. Davina could then find an alternative supplier for the remainder of the period if she wished to. It is worth noting that she does not *have* to terminate the contract, but if she does continue with it, then both parties remain bound to complete all their outstanding obligations.

This chapter has tried to give you a very brief overview of contract law. We have seen how contracts are formed and how they are discharged and had a quick look at remedies, the main one being a claim for compensation to cover any loss incurred by an innocent party who suffers a breach of contract.

Chapter 10 – Core Subjects: Tort

A "tort" is a type of civil wrong. Like contract, it is based largely in common law and therefore made up of the decisions of judges. Also like contract it is a type of civil law and therefore cases are heard in the civil courts such as the County Court and the High Court. A tort is not a criminal offence, although it is possible that the commission of certain criminal offences could lead to an actionable tort, whereby the victim can also sue the perpetrator of the crime for damages (compensation).

The most important tort and one which most people will be aware of is the tort of negligence. This is where someone causes harm to another person due to their carelessness, rather than intentionally. Damage caused to people and property intentionally usually gives rise to a criminal offence of some kind such as assault or criminal damage. However, if it is caused carelessly, then the "victim" must generally seek redress in the civil courts (although some crimes are based on careless behaviour, such as careless driving for example).

If we say that contract law is about agreement then we are really saying that we enter into such relationships voluntarily; if we don't like the contractual terms on offer then we can simply not accept them. Negligence does not require there to be a contractual relationship. If I am driving my car in a careless fashion, then I am potentially liable in negligence if I injure anyone or damage their property. I have not agreed in a contract not to cause that harm or damage, but if I do then I might be liable to the person who suffers.

Negligence was illustrated in the famous case of *Donoghue v Stevenson* (1932). The case also highlights the difference between contractual and tortious liability. Ms Donoghue drank a bottle of ginger beer and became seriously ill due to a decomposed snail in the bottle. As she had not actually purchased the drink (a friend bought it for her), she had no contractual relationship with the seller. She therefore sued the manufacturer directly, who was found liable for negligence. The court said that we all have a duty to take reasonable care not to cause injury or damage to those around us. The manufacturer had breached this duty by allowing a snail to enter the production chain at some point. This caused harm to Ms Donoghue and she was therefore entitled to damages (compensation) from the manufacturer. As I said above, Ms Donoghue could not sue the seller in contract as she had no contract with the seller. She also couldn't sue the seller in tort as the seller had not been negligent (the bottle was opaque and so there was no way for the seller to know that a snail was inside).

Negligence is a complex area of law. Following the *Donoghue* case, there have been many situations in which the law has decided that a duty of care exists between certain people or in certain situations. For example, it is clear to see that a doctor owes a duty of care to her patients, and that a road user owes a duty of care to other road users. Once that duty of care has been breached, then we can say that the person has been negligent. If that negligence then causes harm or loss to the other person, then they can potentially sue for that harm/loss. As in other civil cases, the main remedy would be a payment of money called damages.

There are a couple of "problematic" areas which are worth a mention in relation to negligence. The first is that of pure economic loss. Tort is not generally concerned with such losses, which are more the realm of contract law. If someone causes me economic loss which is not related to any physical harm then my chance of recovery is restricted. One of the leading cases here is *Murphy v Brentwood District Council* (1991), although the facts themselves are a little unhelpful in explaining the concept. Instead, think of a surveyor who values the house I am thinking of buying at £150,000. I later discover that it is actually only worth £120,000. In a way I have lost £30,000, although I have still purchased the thing I thought I was buying. If I had a contract with the surveyor, then I could almost certainly sue him for the difference. However, in tort this would be seen as pure economic loss. Let's say the surveyor was actually instructed by the mortgage company and so I had no contract with him, then I might find that I have no remedy (although see "negligent misstatement below). Another example would be if I negligently caused a traffic delay (say by creating a minor collision), then you could imagine a queue of traffic behind me. Many of those in the queue might suffer economic loss as a result (think of missed business opportunities, shops opening late, job interviews missed and so on). Those people could not sue me for their losses, not least because they are purely economic (they were not actually involved in the crash). To be clear, if I injure someone or cause them other harm, then they can sue me for that, and for any consequential economic loss. If I negligently run you over, then you can claim for your injuries and any losses you might make due to your inability to work for a period of time.

The second "problematic" area of law is to do with psychiatric harm. Once again there is a distinction between such harm which arises as a result of physical harm (or suffered by those who were at risk of physical harm), and that which does not. Much of the law today stems from cases arising from the Hillsborough disaster which occurred at a football ground in Sheffield in 1989. Ninety-six people died in a crush inside the ground, and the psychological impact of the disaster was understandably huge. Claims for psychological harm were brought by people in other parts of the football ground and by those who watched it on television or heard about it in some other way. The leading case is *Alcock v Chief Constable of South Yorkshire Police* (1991). In law, claimants who are not actually in the area of danger are called secondary victims. In *Alcock,* the court decided that such claimants had to pass three tests before it could be said that a duty of care existed. Firstly, they had to have a sufficiently close relationship of love and affection with a victim. Whilst this could be presumed for spouses and parents/children, others would have to prove it. Secondly, there needed to be a proximity to the incident or its aftermath which was sufficiently close in both time and space. Thirdly, the incident needed to be perceived by the person's own senses, rather than say through television or hearing about it from someone else. These tests meant that many of the claims in the Hillsborough case itself failed. Again, remember that here we are talking about people who were not themselves in the area of danger. The normal rules for establishing a duty of care apply to anyone who is.

Another "branch" of negligence is called "negligent misstatement". This is where someone (usually an expert) negligently (carelessly) makes a statement which causes loss to someone else. There generally needs to be a special relationship between the people involved, as in the case of someone giving a reference for another person, or a surveyor acting for a mortgage company who knows their report will be read by the house buyer.

The leading case here is *Hedley Byrne & Co Ltd v Heller & Partners Ltd* (1964). A bank gave a negligent credit reference and, despite no contractual relationship with the recipient of the reference, was potentially liable for the financial loss caused.

Another example of a tort or civil wrong is the law of private nuisance. This generally relates to property. I am entitled to enjoy my property, use it as I see fit and benefit from any rights I might have over it. A private nuisance occurs when someone does something unreasonable to interfere with that enjoyment. Examples would include noise, dust, smoke, tree roots and overhanging branches. If my neighbour allows the roots of her tree to cause damage to my property, then this may well constitute a private nuisance. This is not a crime, but a tort; I should be able to seek compensation in the civil court system if I am the "victim" of such a nuisance.

Another tort which most people have heard of is trespass. We can split this into two categories, being trespass to land and trespass to goods.

Trespass to land is the type of trespass that most people think of when seeing the word "trespass". It covers the situation when a person goes onto land possessed by another person or places something on that land without permission. If I trespass on someone else's land, they can sue me for the tort of trespass, and if they can prove what happened, they would be entitled to damages (compensation). Unlike other torts it is not necessary to show that I have caused the land-owner any loss; the fact that I have trespassed on their land means that the court will make an award of damages.

Trespass to goods, on the other hand, is where I touch, mark or move goods belonging to another. This can be useful when a person interferes with objects which belong to someone else but not in a way that constitutes a criminal offence. For example, if someone borrows my lawn mower fully intending to return it within a short period of time, then technically this may well not be classified as a crime of theft. However, the fact that they have touched, moved and possibly used my possession means I could probably sue them for compensation as a trespass to goods.

Other torts exist such as the tort of conversion (denying ownership of goods to the true owner) but these are rather technical in nature and beyond the scope of an introductory text such as this.

The import thing to remember about torts is that they are civil law mechanisms to provide a remedy to someone who suffers a wrong at the hands of another person. Often there will not be a contractual relationship between the parties, but it is entirely possible that an act could be both a breach of contract and a tort. For example, if a person undertakes a contractual obligation in a negligent fashion, then they could be liable to the "victim" in both contract (for breach of a contractual obligation to act with reasonable skill and care) and in tort (for a breach of the general duty of negligence).

This chapter has given you a brief introduction to the law of torts, covering the law of negligence, nuisance and trespass.

Chapter 11 – Core Subjects: Criminal Law

The criminal law is the area of law which is often most familiar to people who are new to the law. It is the criminal law that we most often read about in the newspapers and see from various perspectives on the television and online.

English criminal law is found in both statutes and case law decisions. The law of murder for example is, as we saw earlier, a common law offence and many of the rules are therefore found in the decisions made by judges over the years as cases have come before them. The rules about theft, on the other hand, are found mainly within the Theft Act 1968, although again there are plenty of relevant case decisions which help us to interpret that Act and establish how it is to be applied to particular sets of facts.

The "body" of criminal law is huge and certainly too large to attempt to list all the offences in this book. Indeed, that is not the purpose of this chapter. Rather this chapter is trying to give you an easy to follow introduction to the subject. I'm sure you could make a fairly lengthy list of criminal offences in any event. They range from serious offences like murder, manslaughter, rape, robbery and blackmail, to burglary, theft, criminal damage and arson, down to often so called "less serious" offences like assault, most driving offences, littering and so on. The list is in fact almost endless when the huge spectrum of minor technical offences is included in the list. My plan in this chapter is to use some interesting examples to help explain what makes criminal law different to the range of varying civil law topics that exist.

Earlier in the book we looked at the differences between civil and criminal law. In particular, we noted the different court systems used by each, and the different remedies or punishments available to those courts. When we looked at tort we saw that to make a successful claim in negligence, for example, a person needs to show that they were owed a duty of care by the wrongdoer, and that the duty was breached, causing harm or damage. In contract law we saw that a contract must first be entered into, following which a breach of contract could be remedied by compensation if the breach caused loss to the innocent party.

Criminal law takes a different approach. Each offence generally has two elements to it. Much as I have tried to avoid using too many technical terms in this book, on this occasion I cannot. The two elements have Latin terms and are known as the actus reus ("act–us–ray–us") and mens rea ("mens–ray–uh") of the offence.

The actus reus of an offence refers to the physical act that constitutes the offence. The mens rea refers to the state of mind that the person committing the offence needs to have to be guilty of the offence.

An example will help to explain these concepts. Let's consider the offence of murder. The actus reus of murder is that I have killed somebody. Therefore, if I harm someone very seriously but they do not die, then I cannot be convicted of murder; I would have to be tried for some other offence such as attempted murder, or grievous bodily harm. The mens rea (state of mind) required for murder is generally the intention to kill or the intention to cause grievous bodily harm (really serious harm). If I deliberately shoot someone and they die then it is likely that I will be convicted of murder; I have killed them and I (presumably) intended to kill them or at least cause them serious harm.

This can be contrasted to the sadly familiar situation in which someone punches or pushes another person, who then falls and hits their head and dies. Whilst this has resulted in a death, and therefore satisfies the actus reus for murder, it is unlikely that the person who threw the punch or did the pushing actually intended to cause serious harm and certainly not to kill. In that case the offence is likely to be manslaughter (the mens rea for manslaughter is complicated by the fact that there are different types of manslaughter, but it usually involves some kind of extreme negligence or recklessness). The important thing to note is that *both* the mens rea and actus reus need to be proved in order for the accused person to be convicted of a crime.

The type of crime which has been committed is crucial because that is what determines the sentence which the judge can give. We saw earlier that serious criminal cases are heard in the Crown Court and that a jury will be present in that court. The jury assess the evidence, such as CCTV pictures, photographs, medical reports, documentary evidence and of course, evidence given by witnesses who come to court to be questioned by lawyers representing the prosecution and the accused. If the jury decided that the accused is guilty then the judge will pass sentence. Murder generally carries a mandatory life sentence, whereas for manslaughter the potential sentence ranges from life in prison to an unconditional discharge (where the offence is recorded but no punishment is given). That reflects the huge range of circumstances and levels of culpability which can result in a charge of manslaughter.

Another good example to consider is the offence of theft, which is set out in the Theft Act 1968. This act contains provisions covering not only theft, but also burglary, robbery, blackmail and taking a vehicle without the authority to name but a few. All these offences have their own characteristics which must be proved before someone can be convicted of that offence. For the purposes of this book we are going to focus on the general offence of theft.

Theft is defined in section 1 of the Theft Act 1968 as follows:

A person is guilty of theft, if he dishonestly appropriates property belonging to another with the intention of permanently depriving the other of it.

This is quite a complex statement and some analysis is required in order to pick out the actus reus and the mens rea for theft. In fact the actus reus is found in the middle of the sentence – "... *appropriates property belonging to another...*" So in order to be guilty of theft I must have appropriated property belonging to another. I can appropriate property by taking it from another person or simply finding it in the street - if I then treat it as my own I have appropriated it. The term property itself is very wide and includes land, buildings and objects as well as things we may not be able to physically touch such as rights. Whether that property belongs to another is usually quite straightforward to determine, although can be complicated when property is owned by one person but in the possession or control of another. Such complexities are beyond the scope of this book; suffice to say that if I take property from someone else it is likely to satisfy the actus reus for theft.

However, as we know, before I can be said to have committed theft, I would need to satisfy the mens rea element of the crime as well as the actus reus element. The mens rea for theft can again be lifted from the basic definition above. The appropriation which is required for theft must be done *dishonestly*, and with the *intention of permanently depriving the other person of the property*. There are two aspects to prove here. Dishonesty is a matter for the jury to decide based on what is expected of reasonable and honest people. If I take a bicycle which I genuinely believe has been abandoned then am I acting dishonestly?

The other aspect of mens rea is that I intend to permanently deprive the other person of the property. Note that this is not part of the actus reus. The test is simply, "was it my intention that the property will never find its way back to the owner?" The test is *not* "did the property find its way back to the owner?" If the latter test applied then I could not be convicted of theft in any case in which the property was recovered. I could steal something and wait to see if I was caught. If I was I could then simply hand the property back and not be guilty of theft. However, the actual position is that when I stole the item I intended to permanently deprive the owner of it, and so I am guilty of theft even if the property is subsequently recovered.

Finally for this chapter, it is worth noting that some offences do not require a mens rea element. These are called "strict liability" crimes and a person is guilty of committing such an offence once they have satisfied the actus reus element. One example is the offence of speeding in a motor vehicle. If I drive at more than 30 miles an hour on a road which is subject to a 30 miles an hour speed limit then I am guilty of the offence of speeding. It does not matter whether I intended to speed, or was reckless as to my speed or even negligent about my speed; the fact that I have allowed my car to speed is enough, and I am guilty of the offence.

I have tried to give you a brief introduction here as to how the criminal law works. We know that cases are heard in the criminal courts, but we have seen here that many offences have two elements to them, the act (actus reus) and the mental element (mens rea). Both need to be satisfied for the crime to be committed, unless it is a strict liability offence which only has an actus reus.

Chapter 12 – Core Subjects: Other areas

There are three other topics which are often included in legal education courses, and certainly in degree courses, which are key to a full understanding of English law. These topics are land law, equity and trusts, and public law. They tend to be more advanced topics and often appear in later parts of courses after topics such as contract law and criminal law have been taught. A further topic, which is often an optional subject in law courses but is vitally important for lawyers, is company law. In this chapter I intend to give a very brief introduction to these topics.

Land law, as you might expect, is about the law relating to land and buildings. One of the most important aspects is about how land can be owned in England and Wales. There are two basic types of ownership, known as freehold and leasehold. If I own the freehold of a property then I own it outright. This can be contrasted to a leaseholder who will have to return the property to the freeholder once the leasehold term expires.

When we talk about leasehold property we do not usually mean a short term lease of a house or business premises. For example, the occupier of a shop may well have leased the shop from its owner. The owner may own the freehold and decide to lease the shop to create a source of income. The occupier will pay a "full market rent" for the right to occupy the shop, which may run to hundreds or thousands of pounds a month. A similar situation occurs when somebody rents a house for a relatively short term, say six months or one or two years; they pay a full market rent to the owner in return for the right to occupy the house. These scenarios create a landlord and tenant relationship which is strictly governed by law, but they are not what we mean when we talk about leasehold land.

If I am buying a house, then I might be able to buy the freehold of the house. That will often depend on whether the seller owns the freehold or not. If they do not, then I might still be able to buy the freehold by finding out who owns it and making them an offer. If the seller does not own the freehold then they are likely to own the leasehold. This means that they own the house on the basis that they have a very long lease of it, often running to as much as 100 years or more. They do not pay a full market rent for the house as we saw with a short lease. Instead, they pay a lump sum for the house in the first place and then a very small rent each year, often running to just a few pounds. When the lease expires, the house would have to be returned to the freeholder, but there are legal protections in place to help the leaseholder in such a case. Many people decide to buy the freehold from the freeholder before the lease expires and this can often be done for just a few hundred pounds.

Another important aspect of land relates to rights over land. This includes such things as rights of way, where someone has a right to enter land and cross it to access land somewhere else, and also charges, where a person grants rights to another person, often in return for a loan. If the loan is not repaid then the person who has the charge can use certain powers to help them obtain repayment of the loan. For example, they might be able to obtain possession of the land and sell it, using the proceeds of sale to reimburse them. Many people buy houses with the aid of a mortgage and this is a type of charge.

Finally, land law also covers the land registration system in England and Wales. The ownership of land (freehold and leasehold) is now registered at HM Land Registry. It is therefore unusual these days to find large bundles of deeds to prove ownership; the land register at the Land Registry contains the information. There are still pieces of land which are not registered in this way but the next time they are sold they will have to be registered.

Moving on to Equity and trusts, this is a subject which tends to cause confusion to those new to the subject. Again it is a topic which is extremely complex. The starting point is probably to understand what we mean by a trust. A trust is where money or property is legally owned by a person on behalf of someone else, perhaps because that other person is not capable of dealing with the money or property in an appropriate way. It requires a rather technical "splitting" of the legal and beneficial ownership. What that means is that if I actually own some money, so that legally it belongs to me, I could place it into a trust whereby I (the "settlor") transfer the legal ownership of the money to someone else, but on the basis that it still actually belongs to me. In other words, that other person is now the legal owner, but I am the beneficial owner. The legal owner, or "trustee", is bound by legal obligations to deal with the money in certain ways, generally ways which will benefit me. The money is said to be held on trust for me. I could direct that the money be held by the trustee for the benefit of someone else. That person would be called a "beneficiary".

Trusts are often found in wills when someone dies. Trustees take ownership of the deceased person's property and hold it on trust for the beneficiaries in the will. For example, if the deceased is leaving money or property to children, then it is often put into a trust until the children reach a certain age, at which time it may be released to them. Another common use for trusts is in the realm of tax planning, whereby people place money into trusts to avoid paying tax or to pay a lower amount of tax. These trusts can sometimes be located overseas.

Public law tends to cover two distinct areas; constitutional law and administrative law.

Constitutional law is about the relationship between the various entities which make up the "state". This includes the executive, the legislative and the judiciary. The executive is basically the government of the day and the entity which decides which laws to make. The legislative is the Parliamentary process which then makes the laws; we looked at this earlier in the book. The judiciary means the court system and so the entity which applies the laws to particular cases. Generally we expect these areas to be separated; something often referred to as the "separation of powers". So, for example, the executive should not interfere with the role of the judiciary. Sometimes we see reports of politicians calling for harsher sentences in specific cases and this is potentially an example of where the powers are not sufficiently separated.

The interesting thing about the constitution in English law is that it is unwritten. Many countries, including the United States of America, have a written constitution which people can read and refer to when asserting their rights. English law has no such document. The issue of human rights is an important part of any constitution and we saw earlier in the book how English law has opened the door to the European Convention on Human Rights by passing the Human Rights Act 1998.

Another important aspect here is the Rule of Law. This dictates that power should not be used arbitrarily (irrationally or without a sound basis), that everyone should be equal before the law (in other words, we are all subject to the law in the same way) and that the constitution is a product of the ordinary law of the land.

Administrative law, which is the other limb of public law, is about the relationship between the state and the individual. In other words, the relationship between the people who live within England and Wales and the State. When we talk about "the State" here, we mean public bodies. This includes bodies which are owned by the state and generally has a fairly wide range. It could, for example, include bodies which are funded by the government.

An important feature of administrative law is a process known as judicial review. This is where a decision made by a public body such as a Local Authority is reviewed by a judge. This might happen because the recipient of the original decision is unhappy with the outcome. The case will be heard in the Administrative Court, which is part of the High Court, and the court has the power, amongst others, to set aside the original decision.

Finally for this chapter, company law is also an important area for lawyers to know something about. A company is a type of business entity which is created by filing certain information at Companies House, which is located in Cardiff in Wales. Once formed, a company takes on a legal personality of its own as confirmed in the famous case of *Salomon v A Salomon & Co Ltd* (1897). That means it can do some things which real people can do. For example, it can enter into contracts, employ people, own property, sue another person and be sued in its own right. It is an artificial person if you like.

The important point here is that it is separate from the people who own it. A company is owned by its shareholders. When I set up a company I invest money into it and in return it issues shares to me. These shares are evidence that I own the company and they therefore have a value; I can sell them to someone else, who would then own the company. I could sell half my shares to someone else and then we would own half the company each. As the value of my company increases, so too does the value of my shares.

The fact that a company is a separate legal person means that it is liable for its own debts. If a company owes me money, I can sue the company in court if it does not pay me. However, I cannot sue the individual shareholders who own the company; the debt is one which is owed by the company, not by them personally.

The other important role in a company along with the shareholders is that of the directors. The directors of the company are actually employees of the company (although they may also own some shares which would make them shareholders too). Directors have day to day responsibility for running the company on behalf of its owners (the shareholders). They have various duties which are set out in the Companies Act 2006 and in particular a duty to act in the best interests of the company for the benefit of the shareholders as a whole. If we think of a large organisation like a bank or a supermarket, we find a small number of directors running the company on behalf of possibly millions of shareholders, all of whom own a small piece of the company. The vast majority of those shareholders have little say in how the company is run, so they rely on the statutory duties to ensure it is being run for their benefit. If they are not happy with the performance of a particular director, they can potentially vote to remove that director, but that will require a majority vote which might be difficult to co-ordinate in such a huge company. In smaller companies shareholders tend to have a much greater say in the running of the company. In fact, in very small companies, the shareholders and directors tend to be the same people.

This chapter has provided a very brief introduction to some of the other main legal topics such as land law, equity and trusts, public law and company law. Many other topics are often covered as optional subjects in law courses, such as employment law, commercial law, environmental law, planning law, the law of finance and so on, but such topics are necessarily beyond the objectives of a book in the "Really Basic Introduction" series.

List of Cases

Alcock v Chief Constable of South Yorkshire Police (1991) – Set the tests for a claim for pure psychiatric harm, page 80.

Alder v George (1964) – An example of the golden rule of statutory interpretation, page 51.

Balfour v Balfour (1919) – An agreement made in a social or domestic setting is generally not legally binding, page 68.

Brock v DPP (1993) – An example of the need for statutory interpretation, page 50.

Currie v Misa (1875) – A case in which the court defined consideration as a benefit to one party or a detriment to the other, page 66.

Donoghue v Stevenson (1932) – Illustrated to the tort of negligence, page 77.

Esso Petroleum Co. Ltd v Commissioners of Customs and Excise (1976) – The parties to an agreement made in a business or commercial setting are generally deemed to intend to be legally bound by that agreement, page 69.

Fisher v Bell (1960) – An example of the literal approach to statutory interpretation, page 51.

Hedley Byrne & Co Ltd v Heller & Partners Ltd (1964) – a case about negligent misstatement, page 81.

Hong Kong Fir Shipping Limited v Kawasaki Kisen Kaisha (1962) – Introduced the concept of innominate terms, page 74.

Murphy v Brentwood District Council (1991) – Pure economic loss is generally not recoverable in tort, page 78.

Pharmaceutical Society of Great Britain v Boots Cash Chemists (Southern) Limited (1952) – A display of goods in a shop is not an offer, page 65.

R v R (1992) – It is an offence for a man to rape his wife, page 46.

Salomon v A Salomon & Co Ltd (1897) – A company has a separate legal personality from its shareholders, page 97.

Smith v Hughes (1960) – An example of the mischief rule of statutory interpretation, page 52.

Taylor v Caldwell (1863) – An example of the doctrine of frustration, page 70.

List of Statutes

Further Reading

To a large degree, what you decide to read next will depend on the reason you are reading about law. If it is for personal interest, then hopefully there are particular areas which you can use as a "search tool" to find further reading which is specific to those topics. If you want to take the next step and increase your level of knowledge and understanding, then you might decide to look for a good A-Level text book or an undergraduate text book on "The English Legal System" – there are plenty of them and they are easily findable in good bookshops or online.

If you want to study law, then I would recommend an A-Level in law to see how you find it. If you want to study for a degree and a traditional University is not an option for you, you could try the Open University, which runs an excellent law degree which is open to everyone, regardless of current qualifications.

Printed in Great Britain
by Amazon